WHEN I GROW UP, I WANT TO FEEL GOOD

How to achieve happiness and understand the world around us

Floren Verdú

Illustrator: Samuel Garrido

INDEX:

Chapter 1:

THE COMFORT ZONE

Once upon a time, there was a country called the Land of Happiness. In this country, many people lived, but I'm going to introduce you to the main characters.

Let me introduce you to Mary and Anthony. Both of them were 8 years old and were siblings. Their dad was named James, and their mom was Charlotte.

On one hand, James was an expert in animals and plants, and on the other hand, Charlotte was an expert in writing and telling stories for boys and girls.

In this country, all the boys and girls went to school, although their school was very different from yours. They only studied how to be happy and how to understand the world around them.

As for Mary, she was a very optimistic and confident girl, but Anthony was quite the opposite. He was a very insecure boy and a bit pessimistic.

Luckily, Mary and Anthony's mom and dad loved them very much and worked hard to make them happy.

One day, the whole family decided to go for a walk in the countryside. Right at the entrance to the palace of the king of the Land of Happiness, there was a sign that said: "I need help getting my falcon to fly! Experts wanted."

James, Anthony and Mary's dad, approached one of the palace guards to inquire about the announcement.

- "Can I request an audience with the king? I would like to help," said James.
- "Wait a moment, I'll call him on the phone." The king says yes, you can come in, but your family will have to wait in the guest lounge," said the royal guard.

James and his family entered the palace. The father went to find the king, while the rest of the family went to the guest lounge.

- "Good morning, Your Majesty! What seems to be the problem with the falcon?" said James.
- "Good day, James! The problem is quite simple. I paid a lot of money for this falcon because they promised me it would fly very high and very fast. However, I can't get it to come down from the same branch. I'm desperate because I've paid the best experts, but

no one has found a solution," said the king.

- "Your Majesty, I think I have the solution. May I proceed with what I have in mind?" said James.
- "Yes, go ahead," said the king.
- "Your Majesty, I'm simply going to cut the branch of the tree, and let's see what happens," said James.

James cut the branch of the tree, and suddenly, the falcon started to fly very high and very fast. The king was very surprised and thanked James.

James and his family returned home, and on the way, he told his family what he had done.

DID YOU KNOW?

The falcon, from the beginning, was very fast and could fly very high, but it didn't want to fly because it was very comfortable in its comfort zone.

What is the comfort zone?
It's that space where we feel comfortable doing activities that we already know and master. It's where the number of surprises is small, and it's very difficult for failure to occur.

How can I leave the comfort zone?
You should set new challenges for yourself and face your fears. **Never forget that you can improve anything you set your mind to.**

Did you know that many people have managed to step out of their comfort zones and have achieved very important things?

Steve Plain.

In 2014, Australian Steve Plain broke his spine. Doctors told him he probably wouldn't walk again, but he promised himself that he would recover and climb the world's 7 most famous summits. After 4 years, he set a record by completing the ascent of the highest mountains on each continent in just 117 days. Impressive!

Bethany Hamilton.

A Hawaiian surfer who lost her left arm when she was only 13 years old due to a shark attack. Learning to swim with one arm wasn't easy, but she returned to competition and managed to rank among the top 50 in the world.

Chapter 2:

THE INNER LIGHT

The school year began, and Mary and Anthony went to their school. Since it was the first day, their teacher, Isabel, decided to take them on a field trip. When they arrived, they saw an elderly man carrying two buckets of water.

It caught their attention that one bucket was new, and the other was very old, causing the old bucket to lose a lot of water along the way.

- "Excuse me, sir, can I ask you a question?" Anthony inquired.

- "Of course, go ahead," the old man replied.
- "Why are you carrying a broken bucket? Don't you have money to buy a new one?" Mary asked.
- "I do have money to buy a new one, but I don't mind that it's broken," the old man responded.
- "I don't understand," Anthony said.
- "It's quite simple. Have you noticed which side of the road the flowers grow on? Do you think, if I didn't lose half the water on each trip, there would be such beautiful flowers here? Let me tell you a secret: did you know that my broken bucket once asked me to throw it away because it didn't feel useful? But I told it no because, just like people, we all have qualities, and my broken bucket is simply different," the old man explained.

Mary and Anthony returned home from school and told their dad and mom what had happened with the old man. So, Charlotte, the mother of the two siblings, took the opportunity to share a little story.

- "All of us have a candle inside us, and it's up to us whether it goes out or stays lit. When we do good deeds, our candle gains strength and burns brighter. But when we do bad deeds, our candle loses strength and can even go out. What do you think the old man was doing with his candle? Lighting it or extinguishing it?" Charlotte asked.

- "Lighting it!" Anthony and Mary exclaimed simultaneously.

DID YOU KNOW?

"The Broken Mirror" by Pedro Pablo Sacristán

A very smart and wealthy boy had the best toys money could buy, and he could get whatever he wanted. One day, he asked his parents to buy him an old mirror. The boy looked at himself in the mirror every day, but he always looked serious, no matter what he did, as he appeared sad.

The boy couldn't understand it and thought the mirror was broken. A few days later, he decided to go out and buy sweets and toys to make himself happy and look in the mirror again, but it still didn't work. Finally, he decided to forget about the mirror and continue with his usual life. On his way to a store, he met a crying child who had lost his parents. The young boy took the child to buy some treats to comfort him.

For a long time, they searched for the child's parents, and eventually, they found them. When the rich and smart boy returned home, he was very surprised because the mirror was radiating a lot of light. It was his inner light reflecting through the mirror.

So, from that moment on, the boy knew what to do whenever he wanted to see the mirror shine.

Just like with the water bucket, being old or ancient doesn't mean something isn't useful, because all people, regardless of their age, have qualities. Nowadays, many retirees participate in volunteer activities, which makes them feel useful to society. Helping others is not a matter of age; it's simply about keeping your inner light alive.

Chapter 3:

GIFTS AND TALENTS

Anthony and Mary, like every day, went to school to continue learning about happiness and understanding the world. Today's lesson involved sprint races, but not all the children had the same ability to run. In fact, there was a girl named Miriam, who had difficulty moving because of her limp. However, she excelled in swimming because her leg was unaffected in the water. Some children laughed at her, but the teacher quickly intervened.

- "Do you think you can measure a fish's ability by its capacity to climb a tree? Can we say a fish is dumb or useless because it can't climb a tree?" the teacher asked.

- "No, the fish simply has different abilities," Mary replied.

- "The same goes for Miriam," added Anthony.

The children who had laughed at Miriam apologized, and everything continued as usual.

When Anthony and Mary returned home, they told their dad and mom about what had happened with Miriam. Meanwhile, James took the opportunity, as his wife was not around, to tell a story to Anthony and Mary.

- "Sit down; I want to tell you a story," James said.

   "A knowledgeable person decided to cross from one island to another by boat and looked for a boatman to take him.

The boatman initially refused to take him because it seemed like a storm was coming.

- 'Have you studied meteorology? How do you know there will be a storm?' asked the intellectual.
- 'I just know from my years of experience,' said the boatman.
- 'Well, you've missed out on part of your life,' said the intellectual.
- The boatman decided not to argue with the intellectual and took him across.
- 'Did you calculate what percentage of your monthly salary you'll earn from this trip?' asked the intellectual.
- 'No, I have no idea,' replied the boatman.
- 'So, you haven't studied accounting either?' asked the intellectual.
- 'No, I could hardly go to school,' said the boatman.

- 'Well, you've missed out on part of your life,' said the intellectual.
- 'Do you see that tree over there? Can you tell me what kind of tree it is?' asked the intellectual.
- 'No, I have no idea,' replied the boatman.
- 'So, you haven't studied botany either?' inquired the intellectual.
- 'No, like I said, I could hardly go to school,' said the boatman.
- 'Sir, we are in the middle of a storm,' said the boatman.
- 'How do you know if you don't understand anything about meteorology?' asked the intellectual.
- 'I just know,' said the boatman.
- 'Do you know how to swim?' asked the boatman to the intellectual.
- 'No,' replied the intellectual.

- "Then you've just lost your life," said the boatman."

- "Did you like the story?" asked James.
- "Yes, I liked it, although I think the intellectual thought he was better than others," said Anthony.
- "I agree with my brother because nobody is better than anyone. We all have things to learn," said Mary.

DID YOU KNOW?

The intellectual believed that being very clever allowed him to disrespect others and make fun of people who knew less than he did. However, we must respect all people because nobody is better than anyone else, as each person has different qualities. Moreover, depending on the activity we are doing, some people will have an easier or harder time. Remember that we can't measure a fish's ability by its capacity to climb a tree. In school, your level will typically be measured in Math and Language, as well as in other subjects where you have to memorize facts. However, if you don't excel in these subjects, don't worry because you can excel both inside and outside of school in the following skills:

- Photography.
- Drawing.
- Music.
- Sports.

- Dance.
- Leadership.
- Studying flora and fauna.
- Human psychology (understanding people).
- Innovation (creating artistic products).
- Entrepreneurship (creating new jobs).
- Knowing and controlling your body (yoga, meditation, etc.)

As you can see, there's no need to worry because we all have gifts and talents.

Chapter 4:

PERSEVERANCE AND HUMILITY

- "Mary and Anthony, your father has a job to study animals on an island near the Land of Happiness. Would you like to go with him, or do you prefer to stay here with me?" Charlotte asked.

- "Mom, I'd like to go with Dad so I can explore a new place," said Anthony.

- "I want to go too," said Mary.

- "No problem at all; both of you can go with your dad," Charlotte said.

James was delighted when he learned that Mary and Anthony would accompany him on the trip. The brother and sister had to ask for permission at school, but their teacher had no objections. During the journey, they took a plane and a boat until they finally arrived on the island. It was beautiful, filled with animals, plants, and crystal-clear water.

The next day, their father went to work, and they were left alone because they were very responsible. From the window of their countryside house, they saw an elderly man tending to a field, but the field was completely empty.

- "Hello, sir," Mary and Anthony said.

- "What a shame that nothing is growing!" exclaimed Anthony.

- "It seems like very infertile land," Mary added.

- "Hello! What do you mean it's not fertile land? On the contrary, I've been planting for 7 years, and soon the fruits of my labor will show," the farmer said.

The two siblings went along with the farmer, thinking he had lost his mind. Shortly after, Anthony and Mary returned to their countryside house.

Three days later, they had to return home, so they decided to bid farewell to the farmer. However, they were very surprised because numerous plants had started to sprout in the field.

- "Mr. Farmer, what's happening here? We thought you had lost your mind," Mary said.

- "That's true, I thought the same," Anthony added.

- "Sit down, and I'll explain. The Japanese bamboo, during the first 7 years of its life, focuses on forming its roots underground. Then, in just 6 weeks, it bursts out of the ground and can grow up to 30 meters or even more," the farmer explained.

- "We apologize," said Mary and Anthony.

- "Don't worry; it was hard to understand," the farmer reassured them.

Anthony and Mary returned home and told their father what they had discovered because they were very excited.

- "Dad, we didn't know that Japanese bamboo was so special, and we discovered it today," Mary said.

- "We love learning about animals and plants," Mary and Anthony added.

On the way to the port, they saw a beautiful garden full of plants, and on one side of the garden, there was a beautiful rose. Near the rose, there was a toad that never left its side. From a distance, James, Mary, and Anthony overheard a conversation between two adults.

- "What a beautiful flower. It's a pity that the toad won't stay away from it," the first adult said.

- "Yes, it's a shame because the presence of that toad ruins the beauty of the rose," the second adult said.

James, Mary, and Anthony heard the entire conversation, although they chose not to intervene. But they were a bit surprised by the unkind words.

In the end, they took a boat and then a plane to return home. Their mother was very happy to see them.

The following week, their father, James, had to return to the island to finish a job, but this time, Mary and Anthony stayed at home with their mother because they couldn't miss more school. When he arrived, James received two surprises. First, the Japanese bamboo had grown significantly, and second, the toad was no longer by the rose, and it was very withered.

- "What happened to you, Rose? You were so beautiful. And where is your friend, the toad?" James asked.

- "I told the toad to leave because he was very ugly, and I am very pretty. I was afraid that people would stop coming to see me. But I didn't realize that I was beautiful because the toad was eating all the bugs around me. I made a big mistake, and now I'm dying," the rose said.

- "I'm sorry, Rose. You should have treated your friend, the toad, better," James said.

When James returned home, he told Anthony and Mary what he had seen. They were happy about the Japanese bamboo's growth but very sad about what had happened to the toad and the rose.

DID YOU KNOW?

Do you think Japanese bamboo is just standing still for 7 years?

Although it may appear to be dormant to the outside world, it's actually strengthening itself to support its growth.

Sometimes in our lives, we start something that excites us, and when we don't see the expected results as quickly as we'd like, we lose motivation and abandon it. Therefore, it's crucial to give time time and not let obstacles defeat us.

I'll tell you some interesting facts about Japanese bamboo:

1. It's the fastest-growing plant in the world.
2. It can grow up to over 30 meters in height.
3. It can grow in forests and plantations.
4. It's stronger than wood and can bend without breaking.

5. It can grow at altitudes of 4,000 meters.
6. Even if you cut it, it will grow again.

Japanese bamboo, just like children, knows how to prepare for success. If misfortune befalls it, it can start almost from scratch because its strength lies in the roots.

"I trained for 4 years to run 9 seconds. Some people, because they don't see results in two months, give up and quit. Sometimes failure is self-inflicted." - Usain Bolt

This quote was said by Usain Bolt, a sprinter with 11 world titles and 8 Olympic titles.

Rushing is not good; it makes us nervous, angry, seek quick fixes, give up when something is about to happen, and also live with anxiety. We need to live with perseverance, meaning we must be consistent in everything we do.

In this chapter, you've also learned about the importance of humility and tolerance.

What is humility?

It's knowing our weaknesses and limitations. Humility is also remembering that no matter how good you are at something, even if you're the world champion, there will always be someone who will be better than you someday. Humility is not bragging about how good you are to people; they already know. Therefore, the rose should have treated the toad well because we all need help from others. Of course, the rose should have been more tolerant because the toad did no harm, in fact, quite the opposite.

What is tolerance?

It's respecting people, their opinions, and attitudes, even if they don't match ours. Finally, the rose should have never forgotten that friendship is more important than the criticisms of strangers.

Chapter 5:

THE POWER OF WORDS

"It was the weekend, and Charlotte wanted to take her family to visit her mom and dad. His name was Joseph, and he was 85 years old, while she was named Anna and was 80 years old. They both lived together in a nearby village in the Land of Happiness.

To get to Grandpa Joseph and Grandma Anna's village, they took a bus, and they had a very fun journey. However, they experienced a somewhat strange situation. A boy who was around 12 years old was moving around on the bus and kept asking his dad questions...

- "Dad, what color are the clouds?" asked the boy.
- "Sweetie, they are white," Dad replied.
- "What's the name of the vehicle we're on?" the boy asked.
- "It's a bus," Dad replied.
- "Does the bus drive itself?" the boy asked.
- "No, it's driven by a driver," Dad replied."

When the bus was stopped at a bus stop, the boy quickly ran to talk to the driver. At that moment, an office worker on his way to work spoke to the boy's father.

- "Sir, have you noticed that your son behaves like a much younger child? You should take him to the doctor," said the office worker.
- "Sir, we've just come from the best doctor in the world. My son had a

cornea transplant, and this is the first time he's seeing the world I've told him about so many times," replied the boy's father.

-

The office worker was very surprised by the answer and apologized to the boy's father. Meanwhile, our favorite family in the story stayed quiet and didn't want to get involved.

Charlotte, James, Anthony, and Mary arrived at the home of Grandpa Joseph and Grandma Anna and quickly went to greet them.

Anthony and Mary said hello to their grandparents and couldn't resist telling them what had happened on the bus.

- "Words can be the best or the worst," said Grandpa Joseph.

- "Let me guess, are you going to tell them the story of words?" Grandma Anna asked.
- "You're right, you know me well," said Grandpa Joseph.

- "Once upon a time, there was a leader of a country who spoke very unkindly to his people. He sent a servant to buy meat at the market and asked him to bring the best piece of meat. But the servant bought an old, fly-covered tongue instead. The master ate it and thought he would scold the servant later. Surprisingly, the food was good. Another day, he sent him to the market and told him to bring the worst piece of meat, and the servant brought the same tongue again. The servant told his master that he had followed the order because the tongue could be the best or the worst. If you used good words, it would be sweet and bring happiness. However, if you used bad words, it would be tough and bitter, causing anger, rage, and sorrow.

The kind-hearted leader understood that he had been given a lesson. The next day, he gathered his people and asked for forgiveness," said Grandpa Joseph.

- "Grandpa, I really liked the story," said Anthony.
- "The bus office worker didn't use words nicely at first, but then he used them correctly to apologize," Mary pointed out.
- "That's right, but his words had already hurt the boy's father. We should think before we judge," said Grandpa Joseph.

DID YOU KNOW?

The bus office worker thought that the 12-year-old boy wasn't well and needed a doctor because he was behaving like a very young child. However, for the boy, it was the first time he had contact with the world.

This story teaches us that it's not a good idea to judge people. Before you judge, remember that everyone has their own story. We often think about things we don't know, create our own thoughts, and judge others without knowing them. We might say, "If I were in their shoes, I would do things differently," but you're not that person, and you're not in the same situation. Before you judge or get angry with someone, make sure you know their story; you might be surprised.

When the bus office worker talked to the 12-year-old boy's father, his words hurt him because the office worker shouldn't have said anything. He should have just observed, like our main family did. The words he used, even though not unkind, hurt the father, but he wasn't upset because he was very happy since his son was seeing for the first time.

Never forget that words have a lot of power because it's not the same to say...

"You don't want to spend time with me anymore, do you?"

As saying...

"I miss you; I'd like to see you more."

The reaction will be different.

Chapter 6:
THE TWO BUTTONS

The school year was quite advanced, and the teacher decided to surprise the students in her school. However, it wasn't going to be a pleasant surprise because she had decided that, for a week, they would operate like a traditional school. This meant they would have classes like English, Math, Natural Sciences, Social Studies, and more.

Mary and Anthony didn't understand the teacher's decision because in the Land of Happiness, classes were all about working on happiness and understanding the world to try to make it better.

When they got home, they ran to talk to Charlotte and James.

- "Dad, Mom, I'm really nervous; I don't want to have those subjects," said Anthony.
- "What subjects?" asked James.
- "English, Math, Natural Sciences, and Social Studies," said Anthony.
- "Me neither, because we'll have to do homework and study. But I think the teacher is doing it so we can learn new things," said Mary.
- "That's right, Mary, you have to be positive," said Charlotte.
- "I'm not going to school; you won't convince me," said Anthony.
- "Son, don't be negative; you're hitting the panic button," said Charlotte.
- "But what button? What are you talking about?" asked Anthony.
- "When we have a problem, it's up to us to decide how we react. We have two buttons: the panic button and the solution button. Depending on which button we press, we'll turn into a

superhero or a mountain. The panic button will be the black one, while the solution button will be the green one. If we complain about the new situation, we'll be hitting the black button and turn into a mountain. So, we'll stay stuck in front of the problem. If we stay calm and press the solution button, the green one, we'll put on our superhero or superheroine outfit and can find a solution to our problem. Depending on the button we press, our attitude will be one or the other," said Charlotte.

- "Which button do you want to press?" asked James.
- "The green one," answered Mary.
- "And you, Anthony?" asked Charlotte.
- "The green one, because it's more fun to be a superhero than a mountain," Anthony replied.

-   "Anthony, I really liked your answer," said James.

The next day, both siblings went to school and had their first classes, but as these subjects were new, the first mistakes came.

When they got home, Mary was worried because she had made some mistakes in her Math exercises, while Anthony wasn't very happy because he had received low grades in Natural Sciences.

-   "Mary, what I told your brother about problems also applies to mistakes, like the ones you made in your Math exercises. It even applies when we face an obstacle that we don't like but have to overcome, for example, having to take new subjects at school," said Charlotte.
-   "Mary, which button will you press? Green or black?" Charlotte asked.

- "The green one, Mom, I'm a superheroine," replied Mary.

Charlotte and Mary sat together and corrected all the Math exercises that were wrong. While correcting the exercises, Mary realized that Math wasn't as hard; she just needed to put in effort and have a good attitude.

- "Dad, I don't like Natural Sciences; they're boring!" said Anthony.
- "Anthony, getting low grades doesn't mean they're boring or difficult; it means you haven't tried hard enough. Right now, you have an obstacle in front of you, and you have to decide which button to press. Remember that Dad is an expert in animals and plants and can help you if you choose the right button," said James.

- "Dad, I choose the green button; it's very boring to be a mountain because I'd have to stay still," said Anthony.

From that very day, Anthony began to take an interest in animals and plants, and when he had the Natural Sciences subject, he didn't see it as an obstacle but as an opportunity to learn new things.

As time went on, the teacher continued to teach her classes in Math, English, and Sciences. In general, the boys and girls were not happy and started making unkind comments about the teacher.

Anthony had heard one comment that he found very unpleasant, so he ran to tell her.

- "Miss Isabel, I want to tell you something I've heard about you," said Anthony.
- "Have you asked yourself the three questions?" the teacher asked.

- "What questions?" asked Anthony.
- "Are you sure that what you're going to tell me is true?"
- "No, I don't have any proof," Anthony replied.
- "Is it good?" the teacher asked.
- "No, quite the opposite," Anthony replied.
- "Is it necessary to tell me?" the teacher asked.
- "I don't think it is," Anthony replied.
- "Then, if it's not true, not good, and not necessary, why should we waste time on it?" Miss Isabel said.

This way, the teacher never found out that they were saying she was a witch who flew every night on a broomstick and cast spells to turn animals into boys and girls.

DID YOU KNOW?

The brother is good at some things, and the sister is good at others. So, it's the same as what happens to you and your classmates.

Mary and Anthony would love to spend the day doing the things they love the most because their life would be very easy. But sometimes, they encounter small problems, face obstacles, and occasionally make mistakes. When this happens, the situation can get really tough.

With practice, you'll remember to press the green button. Sometimes the solution will be to ask for help or wait a little to find a solution. With the superhero or superheroine outfit, you'll feel better, and it will be worth trying to find a solution. When we don't stop until we find a solution, that's called perseverance.

Sometimes, we'll be so nervous and upset that it will be really hard to press the green button. But don't worry because it's not easy, and it happens to adults too. In fact, you'll probably have to help them press the right button.

Remember that when faced with an obstacle, mistake, or problem, we can always choose between seeking a solution or complaining. Seeking a solution will help us move forward and learn, while complaints will leave us stuck.

Which button do you choose? Green or black? I'm clear about it.

Stay away from gossip and unkind comments!

When someone comes to tell us something bad about us, even if they claim it's out of friendship, it hurts us. We quickly feel sad and angry. We might even lose a friend.

Where's the advantage? In negative messages, the messenger is just as guilty as the person who spoke ill of us. Because between the two of them, they make us feel bad. And is that useful for anyone?

Chapter 7:
NEVER GIVE UP

Winter arrived, and some lakes in the Land of Happiness froze, but Anthony and Mary were very happy because they loved playing in the snow, skiing, and skating.

One day, they decided to go fishing at the lake near their house. Since they didn't want to harm the fish, they simply caught them and released them.

While they were fishing, suddenly, the ice started to crack.

- Anthony, we should move to another place; I think the ice is going to break - said Mary.

- I don't think so; the ice is very hard, and we weigh very little - said Anthony.

Unfortunately, the ice broke, and Anthony fell into the water. Anthony got very nervous and ended up under the ice sheet.

Mary could hardly see where her brother was, but she gathered her courage and took a skate from her backpack. So, with the blade of the skate, she began to hit a massive layer of ice. Finally, after a lot of effort, she managed to break it, and with the help of a rope, she managed to pull her brother out.

Quickly, Mary left her brother safely and ran for help.

Several people from their village came to help, but people couldn't stop saying...

- How could she do it?

- It was impossible to break the ice; the layer was too thick.

An elderly man who was nearby approached when he heard the comments.

- I have the solution to the answer; there was no one around to tell her she couldn't - said the old man.

The neighbors accompanied Mary and Anthony back to their house; their mom and dad were scared by what had happened.

James and Charlotte decided to let their two children be and not make too much of the matter, although they obviously took Anthony to the doctor. But fortunately, Anthony was perfectly fine thanks to the bravery of his sister, Mary.

The next day, their mom and dad decided to talk to Anthony and Mary.

- Mary, on behalf of your dad and me, we would like to thank you - said Charlotte.
- That's right, you've been very brave - said James.
- Little sister, I also want to thank you; you helped me out of the ice - said Anthony.
- I didn't have any other choice; you would have done the same for me - said Mary.
- Charlotte, why don't you tell them the story of the deaf frog? - James asked.
- Great idea, James - Charlotte said.
- "Two frogs fell into a well; both of them kept jumping to try to get out. From above, the rest of the frogs shouted and gestured to them not to tire themselves out because it was impossible to get out. One frog gave up and died there from exhaustion and despair.

The other frog kept jumping without stopping until it finally landed on a ledge and from there could jump to another, and finally managed to get out. The other frogs were surprised because this frog had succeeded.

The frog said she was a little deaf, but she had made it thanks to the encouragement of the frogs outside, as she understood that those shouts and gestures were to cheer her on" - Charlotte said.

- "Mom, that frog made it because she was a little deaf; if she had listened, she would have gotten discouraged" - Anthony said.

- "You're absolutely right, Anthony. If someone had been near the lake, your sister wouldn't have managed to rescue you because someone would have told her it was impossible to break the ice" - Charlotte said.

DID YOU KNOW?

Mary managed to save her brother because she fought for her goal and didn't listen to anyone who told her she couldn't achieve it, just like the frog. Because there will always be people who will tell you that you can't do it. You have to believe in yourself and know that with effort and perseverance, you can achieve anything you set your mind to.

"As whether you think you can or you can't, you're right." - Henry Ford.

Who was *Henry Ford*?
He was an American who founded the Ford Motor Company.

Walt Disney worked at a newspaper from which he was fired for a lack of imagination and good ideas.

Albert Einstein was once considered mentally disabled or slow in thinking because he didn't start speaking until he was 4 years old and didn't learn to read until he was 7. Despite his slow start, he went on to win the Nobel Prize in Physics.

Valentina Tereshkova was selected in 1962 and sent into space aboard Vostok 6, becoming the first woman and also the first non-astronaut to travel there.

These individuals always had clear goals and never entertained the idea of giving up because they never listened to the people who told them they couldn't do it.

Never say:
"I can't do it!"

The right thing to say is:
"How can I achieve it?"

No matter how many times you make mistakes, behind each mistake, there is a lesson that will enable you to achieve success.

Never give up!

Chapter 8:

WHERE IS HAPPINESS?

Anthony and Mary, like any other day, went to school, but they noticed that their teacher, Isabel, was sad.

- Miss, what's wrong with you? - asked Anthony.
- My husband has left home - replied the teacher.
- Doesn't he love you anymore? - asked Mary.
- It's not that, Mary, he just went to search for a treasure - replied teacher Isabel.
- How exciting! - exclaimed Anthony.
- Well, I don't find it exciting at all! - exclaimed Isabel.

\- Don't worry, Miss, he'll surely be back soon - said Mary.

David, Isabel's husband, had decided to leave the Land of Happiness and travel 5000 kilometers. During his journey, he had to use various modes of transportation. It took him one month to reach his destination, which was a very distant country called the Land of Darkness.

Under a bridge, David encountered a soldier and quickly told him that he had traveled 5000 kilometers because a magician had told him that he would find a treasure right under that bridge.

The soldier was shocked and told David that he had received the same message from the magician, but the magician had told him that he would find a treasure in the house of a teacher named Isabel in the Land of Happiness.

David was speechless and decided to return home because something strange was happening. This time, David only took three weeks to get back home because he already knew the way.

When he arrived in the Land of Happiness, the first thing he did was go to find his wife and apologize for all the time he had been away from home. He also told her everything that had happened.

David still couldn't make sense of what had happened during his journey, so he went to speak with the wisest person in the Land of Happiness. This person was an elderly man over 100 years old who lived alone in a beautiful village house, and his name was Frank.

- "Mister wise, a magician appeared to me and told me I would find a treasure under a bridge in a place called the Land of Darkness. However, when I got there, I found a soldier under that same bridge, and he told me a magician had said he would find a treasure in my house. I am a little scared and worried," said David.

- "Neither you nor the soldier have understood anything. Let me tell you a story; maybe this way, you'll understand" - said the wise Frank.

- "A woman went from village to village in search of happiness. In each of the villages, she sought out the local sages and said: 'I'm looking for someone who can make me feel complete happiness, and whoever can do that will receive all my money.' But no one was willing to help her. One day, she approached a man meditating under a tree and understood that he was a sage of the place. She told him the same story, and the man got up, took the woman's bag, and ran away. The woman was very sad, thinking she had been robbed.

While searching through the village, she saw another man meditating under a tree, and her bag was next to him. The woman picked up her bag and found that all her money was there. The wise man opened his eyes and asked, 'Are you happy now?' And the woman replied that she had never been so happy." - said the wise Frank.

- "Do you understand the story?" - asked the sage.
- "Yes, happiness is about appreciating the things you have" - replied David.
- "Correct, David. You insisted on going to search for a treasure 5000 kilometers from home, but the greatest treasure was right nearby. It was all about being grateful for everything you had, especially your

family, wife, friends" - said wise Frank.

- "So, the magician was testing me?" - asked David.

- "Exactly, the magician wanted you to value everything you had, and to achieve that, he made you lose almost everything for almost two months, just like the woman in the story, who lost all her money" - said wise Frank.

DID YOU KNOW?

Where is happiness?

The most valuable things in life, our family, friends, and ourselves, are always with us. We often search far and wide for what is very close. **Humans often fail to appreciate things until they are lost.** The strength of feeling grateful for everything we have lies in gratitude.

Happiness can be found in the simplest of things:

- When you make a new friend.
- When you win a game.
- When your teacher praises you or gives you a good grade.
- When your grandparents come to visit and play with you.
- When you receive a gift.
- When you're allowed to sleep over at a friend's house.
- When the girl or boy you like smiles

at you.
- When you're allowed to watch what you like on TV.
- When you're allowed to eat something you really enjoy.

Happiness is found in the little things and in appreciating what you have. Having many toys won't make us happier because we only play with a few. Owning expensive items won't make us happier because an object can't give us a hug.
The most important thing is to love ourselves, remember that the greatest treasure is inside us, and of course, we should spend time with the people who love us.

Chapter 9:

ANGER MANAGEMENT

One more day, Mary and Anthony were returning from school when suddenly they saw a boy and a girl shouting at each other in the middle of the street. Anthony and Mary didn't understand what was happening, but they felt very uncomfortable in that situation and decided not to stop and quickly return home.

- "Mom, Dad, why do people shout when they get angry?" - Mary asked.

- "Mary and I got scared when we saw a couple shouting at each other" - Anthony said.

- "There are several reasons: they lose their temper, they don't know how to control themselves, but most importantly, it's because they distance themselves" - Charlotte said.

- "What do you mean by 'distance themselves'? The person you're shouting at is right there" - Anthony said.

- "Their bodies are close, but their hearts are distant at that moment, and that's why they need to shout louder and louder" - their dad, James, said.

- "The opposite can also happen; two people in love speak softly because their hearts are very close" - Charlotte said.

- "We mustn't let anger grow between people because there may come a point where the distance between their hearts is so great that there's no way back" - James said.

DID YOU KNOW?

Sometimes, when you're a little boy or a little girl, you shout because you don't know how to express your feelings, or maybe you've seen your mom or dad do it. When you realize that shouting gets you what you want, you might keep doing it, but that's not the right way to behave.
We should never shout at people.
What do you think will happen if we walk into a store yelling?
How do you think the salesperson will respond to us?
We need to learn to talk calmly. When we hear shouting at home, we should step away from it because shouting doesn't lead to good communication, and we won't be able to reach an agreement. It's normal to get upset with someone, even with ourselves.

In such situations, when someone has shouted at us:

1. **We won't shout back.**
2. **We'll step away.**
3. **We'll take a deep breath.**

Besides, after we've calmed down, we'll try to find a positive solution to what happened. If it was us who shouted, we should apologize.

The story of the boy and the nails.
"A boy had lots of problems with people because of his bad temper. He asked his father for help, and his dad gave him a hammer and nails.
His dad told him that every time he got angry, he should nail a nail behind the door. At first, he nailed many, but then there was a time he didn't nail any.
The boy was happy and called his dad to say he did it. But his dad told him it wasn't finished. For each day he didn't get angry, he had to remove a nail. Eventually, he took all the nails out. But his dad said the door would never be the same."

We need to be careful about how we treat others because when we hurt someone, the relationship won't be the same, as the damage is done.

So, everything we do has consequences, even if we say sorry later.

We should treat people with respect if we want them to respect us. And we have to control our anger because anger can hurt others and leave lasting marks. It's not just about fixing our mistakes; it's about not hurting people in the first place.
Lastly, we know we'll feel angry at times, but we have to learn to control it so we don't hurt ourselves or the people around us.

Chapter 10:

POSITIVE OR NEGATIVE ATTITUDE

Anthony and Mary had argued in the schoolyard because the teacher had taken a toy from Anthony to give it to Mary. Anthony didn't agree because he thought he had it for a short time, while Mary thought it was her turn.

In the end, they both ended up yelling at each other and saying mean words, so Mrs. Isabel punished both of them by not allowing them to play in the yard, fortunately, only for a while.

On the way back home, they didn't talk and arrived very angry. James and Charlotte saw the situation and decided to talk to both of them.

- "What happened at school? asked Charlotte.

- "Why did you argue?" asked James.

- "The teacher likes Mary more than me," said Anthony.

- "That's not true!" - said Mary.

- "Can someone tell me what happened at school?" - asked Charlotte.

- "I had a toy, and Mrs. Isabel took it from me to give it to Mary"
  - answered Anthony.

- "I wanted to play with the toy my brother had, and he never let me"
  - said Mary.

- "Sit down, both of you" - said James.

- "We're going to explain some things"
  - said Charlotte.

There are two types of frustration:

1. Things aren't always the way we want them to be, but we can't do anything to change them.

2. Things aren't always the way we want them to be, but we can do something to change them.

- When we can't change something, we can choose how we react. Sometimes, we get angry, and we can't help it. Anger is like a black balloon inside us, and if it lasts a long time, the balloon gets bigger.

What can we do when we notice that happening? Breathe. Every time we breathe, the balloon changes color and gets smaller. It will keep changing color until it turns lilac, which is the color of calmness.

Sometimes, we get so angry that it's not easy to start breathing, but we have to remember it's worth it. When we're calm, we can look for a solution or an alternative, and we'll do that by pressing the green button, the solution button.

An alternative is to do an activity that makes us feel better, whatever you decide. It's okay to get angry, but sometimes, no matter how angry you get, you can't change what happened. However, you can decide what to do with the balloon growing inside you. You decide if you want it to get big or start breathing – said Charlotte.

- "What do you prefer, keeping that balloon inside, or breathing and calming down and doing something that makes you feel better?" – asked James.

- "And, above all, you have to avoid the balloon from exploding because if it does, the damage will be irreversible, and you'll hurt people a lot. Do you remember, in the story 'The Boy and the Nail' the door never became the same? Because the holes were already there" – said James.

Mary and Anthony apologized to each other and understood that they hadn't acted in the right way. They realized that problems can't be solved with shouts and anger. So, from that day on, they started thinking about their inner balloon and the green button to find a solution.

DID YOU KNOW?

Children learn more from what they see their parents do than from what their parents tell them. When you want to be happy, it's much easier when you see your mom and dad happy. Children need affection and to be told how much they are loved. Like adults, children also need to be listened to, but remember, yelling won't make you right.

Problems and obstacles will come sooner or later, so you have to prepare yourself to face them. **Our parents should not avoid all problems for us because we have to make mistakes many times, remember, mistakes are great teachers.**

Children, like adults, also have to choose between having a positive or negative attitude. **Don't forget that sometimes you can't choose what happens to you, but you can choose the attitude you take toward what happens.**

Justin Timberlake:

This famous singer-songwriter and actor was diagnosed with ADHD when he was very young. Not only was he rejected by the rest of his classmates, but he also experienced bullying. He faced many challenges, but ADHD didn't stop him from moving forward and becoming a successful worldwide singer.

What is ADHD?

It's a condition that causes attention problems and difficulties controlling impulses. In general, children with ADHD are very active and find it challenging to sit still.

Keira Knightley:

She is an actress known for her role in the movie *"Pirates of the Caribbean."* The English actress and model were diagnosed with dyslexia when she was just 6 years old. However, her passion for acting helped her overcome difficulties in reading. She admitted that her role in this movie motivated her to practice reading and surpass herself.

What is dyslexia?

It's not an illness, as it is a learning disorder. Dyslexia makes it harder for children who have it to read and learn to read because their brains make it challenging. However, they can be very intelligent boys and girls.

Clearly, *Keira* and *Justin* faced significant challenges from a very young age. What attitude did they take toward the problems? Positive or negative? Which button did they press? The green or the black one?

You can't control the problems you'll encounter along the way, but you can control your attitude towards them.

Chapter 11:

WE ARE THE REFLECTION OF OUR PARENTS

Like every weekend, Charlotte, James, Anthony, and Mary decided to go together to do activities, this time they decided to go to the swimming pool in their town, which you already know is in the Land of Happiness. When they arrived, they asked the girl at the ticket booth for 4 tickets.

- Excuse me, can you give us 4 tickets for the pool? - Mary asked.

- Yes, of course, we have two types of tickets, up to 7 years old they are €2, and from 8 years old they are €5 - said the girl at the ticket booth.

- Well then, I want 4 tickets for €5 - said James.

- You could have saved €6; I wouldn't have noticed that your son and daughter were over 7 years old - said the pool employee.

- I know, but he and she would have noticed - said James.

The time has come to say goodbye, but don't be sad because I promise you that Mary, Anthony, Charlotte, and James will be back with more adventures.

DID YOU KNOW?

Charlotte and James wanted Anthony and Mary not to lie, and for this reason, they told the truth to the ticket girl, thus promoting the value of honesty.

What is honesty?
It is a quality that involves respecting others, not stealing, and telling the truth.
Mary and Anthony were fortunate to have a dad and mom who were an excellent example for him and her.

What would happen if your mom and dad were not a good example for you?

Yulimar Rojas.
She is a Venezuelan athlete who was the Olympic champion in triple jump at the 2020 Tokyo Olympics. The jumper was born in one of the humblest neighborhoods of Caracas (Venezuela). Her dad left her and

her family when she was very young, and she and her 6 siblings were raised by her mom. It was very difficult for her to have a meal a day, but she always dreamed of having a better life. She never gave up and managed to escape poverty.

Cristiano Ronaldo.
He is one of the best football players in the world, but his life was not always easy. He was born into a poor family in a neighborhood in Madeira (Portugal).
His father died in 2005, and it is said that he was an alcoholic, making the situation at home very complicated.
For these reasons, he spent most of his time on the street playing football. You know that he ended up becoming a global star.

Even though we are the reflection of our dads and moms, *Yulimar* and *Cristiano* chose the positive example, that is, the example of two determined mothers who did everything possible to make their sons and daughters happy.

So, *Yulimar* and *Cristiano* chose to be happy despite their tough childhoods because it's very easy to be happy when everything is to our liking and we have no difficulties.

Therefore, even though we are the reflection of our mom and dad, if we've had the misfortune of being born into a complicated family, it's not the end.

We can always achieve everything we set our minds to, although it will undoubtedly be more challenging.

RECOMMENDATIONS

I invite you to follow *Anna Morató, Alex Rovira, and Eloy Moreno*. They have been my source of inspiration and are the ones who have allowed me to contribute my little grain of sand through this story. And, of course, I have based it on the Stoic philosophy that has helped me so much in my life.

As for me, this will not be my last book. In fact, this will be the first book in a long series. So, pay attention to Amazon because this book will continue with new stories and lessons.

To conclude, I would greatly appreciate a positive review on Amazon. Thank you very much.

HOW TO CONTACT THE AUTHOR AND ILLUSTRATOR?

Floren Verdú
florenvb@gmail.com
florenvb@hotmail.com

Illustrator: *Samuel Garrido*
samuelgfrances@gmail.com
Instagram contact @samuelgftattoo

Made in the USA
Monee, IL
26 December 2024

4a782653-7bcf-4865-9118-1acce2155656R01